prosciutto
pancetta
salame

prosciutto
pancetta
salame

Text and Recipes by Pamela Sheldon Johns

Produced by Jennifer Barry Design

Photography by Joyce Oudkerk Pool

Ten Speed Press
Berkeley • Toronto

A Kirsty Melville Book

Ten Speed Press
P.O. Box 7123
Berkeley, California
94707

Distributed in Australia by Simon and Schuster Australia, in Canada by
Ten Speed Press Canada, in New Zealand by Southern Publishers Group, in South Africa
by Real Books, and in the United Kingdom and Europe by Airlift Book Company.

Concept and Design: Jennifer Barry Design, Fairfax. California
Production Assistance: Kristen Wurz
Food Stylist: Pouké
Copy Editor: Carolyn Miller

Library of Congress Cataloging-in-Publication Data

Johns, Pamela Sheldon, 1953–
Prosciutto, pancetta, salame / text and recipes by Pamela Sheldon Johns ;
photography by Joyce Oudkerk Pool.
p.   cm.
Includes bibliographical references and index.
ISBN 1-58008-617-9
1. Cookery, Italian. I. Title.
TX723.J6428   2005
641.5945—dc22   2004023014

First printing, 2004

Printed in China
1 2 3 4 5 6 7 8 9 10 — 07 06 05 04

contents

introduction

"*Signora, sono io, qui per respirare l'aria del posto dove sono nata.*" ("Signora, it is I, here to breathe the air of the place I was born.")

Signora Roghi comes to visit me each spring on her birthday. She is always very sentimental, emotional, and full of stories about her life as a child on my farm. "That's my grandmother." She points to a photo hanging on my wall. "Inside that barn is where we kept the chickens and some farm tools." She is talking about my dining room. In the days when she lived here, all of the downstairs level was for the animals. The pigs lived in what is now my kitchen, the cow in what is now my office. Some of the old farm implements remain. One is a large kettle that was used to heat the food for the pigs in the winter.

In the past, farmers would often raise one pig each year. In the late fall or early winter, it would be butchered and turned into the products that would nourish and sustain the family throughout the year. This guaranteed a supply of meat not only through the winter, but also for the warmer months, when spoilage was a problem. Every part of the animal was used. First, the large cuts to be cured whole were prepared: the leg, the shoulder, the loin, and the belly. The smaller bits and pieces were chopped with fat, seasoned, and stuffed into casings. The remaining fat was cured to be used as a flavoring for beans or soups. The internal organs and the blood were ingredients for rich sausages that were a winter staple, along with all of the odd parts, the head included, which were cooked and pressed into a product known in America as head cheese. In Tuscany it is called soppressata. Similar products are found in other regions by different names: testa in cassetta from Liguria and Piemonte; marcundela of Friuli-Venezia Giulia; bondòla from the Veneto; zeraria in Liguria; coppa di testa of Marche; mustardela from Piemonte; and soppressata, biroldo, or buristo in Tuscany.

"I have fond memories of eating the fresh pork when the pig was killed," Signora Roghi remembers. "It was a kind of a feast day; then we had the work of putting up the rest."

The term *salumi* is generic, covering the range of cured meats from sausages to large pieces of meat such as *prosciutti*. *Salumi* evolved as a way to preserve meats in a time when there was no refrigeration. In Italy, most of the meat used in *salumi* is pork, but some products are also made with beef, goat, horse (still popular in bresaola and salame in the northern regions), boar, deer, sheep, goose, or donkey.

In a country that has been united for just over a hundred years, the variations on technique and names of *salumi* can be mind-boggling. Some products are made in a tiny valley with only a couple of producers, while some are found across the country. Some made identically have different names in other regions. Some with the same name are made in completely different ways. When considering the varieties of cured meats in Italy, we should remember the diversity of climate, geography, economy, and regionality. The cultural acceptance and regionality of certain types of cured meats evolved before refrigeration and are maintained today as a matter of taste. Climate certainly influenced this; for example, the north is cooler and moister, and the cured meats from that area include large pieces such as a whole leg of pork (prosciutto). In the south, it is too hot for large pieces of meat to cure without spoiling.

Another significant difference between the north and south is the use of spices. Traditionally, the south uses more *peperoncino*, or hot red pepper, and the north tends to employ sweeter flavors. This, too, may be due to the climate. Spicy flavoring may have been used to cover off flavors that developed in the hot temperatures. The use of different spices may have also been historically influenced by the spice trade and the relative wealth of the north.

Changes in culture have influenced the rise and decline in the existence of products as well. A good example is a salame from Piemonte called bale 'd'aso. In local dialect, the name literally translates to "donkey's testicles," and this salame may have included those at one time, but now the name only refers to the shape. The use of donkey meat dates back to the time when much commerce was done with donkey-drawn caravans. Now that trucks have replaced the carts, donkey meat is not as abundant, and the salame is cut with 60 percent pork and 20 percent beef. And, with the advent of modern transport, products have now found their way outside of their historic production area and into the supermarkets of other regions.

◆

The two main categories of *salumi* are cured whole meats and *incassati*, chopped pieces in casings. The butcher starts by cutting and preparing the prime cuts. In the case of pork, the hind legs are usually set aside for prosciutto, the famed raw cured ham. The shoulder and loin are cured in a similar way and are

Pliny the Elder, a Roman historian from the first century A.D., explained the popularity of pork when he said, "From no other animal can man draw more material for gluttony: pork has almost fifty different flavors, whereas other animals have only one."

called spalla and lombo, respectively. Pancetta, the secret ingredient in many Italian recipes, comes from the fat of the belly (*pancia* is Italian for "belly") and can be compared to bacon, except that it is usually not smoked. Every region has a form of prosciutto, spalla, lombo, and pancetta. Even though they are created by a similar process, some are markedly different in flavor, such as the sweet prosciutto di Parma or prosciutto di San Daniele of Friuli-Venezia Giulia, the salty Tuscan prosciutto, and the smoked boneless speck from Trentino–Alto Adige.

The *incassati* are the parts that haven't been cured in large pieces; they are chopped, seasoned, and placed in casings. Fresh sausage is made with ground pork and bits of fat that may be seasoned with garlic, salt, and spices and stuffed into casings. These sausages, when aged, become salame (the Italian spelling, called salami in the United States). The classic salame is usually 3 to 4 inches across and in varying lengths. Depending on the traditions of the region, variations include different meats, seasonings, lengths, and shapes. The size of the diameter is determined by the casings. Lamb casings are much smaller than cow casings, for example.

Quality and taste come initially from four factors: breeding, nutrition, the health and well-being of the animals, and butchering. Forty to fifty years ago, there was a trend toward replacing the historic breeds with newer breeds that grew more quickly, were leaner, were more fertile, and had other marketable qualities. However, some consumers noticed the decline in taste and quality, and they began to demand a return to the traditional breeds. In many areas, this has become a priority and has met with great success.

More attention is now being paid to the way the animals are raised. In some cases, the diets are augmented with the kind of food they would have eaten in the past, such as acorns and chestnuts. Care is taken to be sure that the animals are not stressed in their environment; that they have enough space; and that, when transported, the conditions are well ventilated and of a reasonable temperature. We are beginning to discover that integrity of flavor and the impact on human nutrition in the meats, as well as disease resistance and abundant reproduction in the animals, can be encouraged with good handling. The best results come from producers where these factors are considered, excessive daily growth is not encouraged, and growth hormones are not used.

curing

Curing is the complex process of transforming fresh meat to a meat product that can be stored over a period of time. It is an ancient art that evolved over the centuries, with its origins in early Egypt and China. The Germans, Celts, and Romans continued and developed the practice. Cured meats supplied men on ships, nomads, and shepherds moving their animals to and fro with a transportable protein.

In Italy, techniques of curing meats have been handed down from generation to generation. The three major methods of curing are salting (or brining), air-drying, and smoking. Cooking can be a method of preservation as well, but is less common. Sometimes, a combination of two or three of these methods is used. Each region of Italy has its own historic version of how the meats are prepared, derived from the types of raw materials available and the climate.

types of salumi/regional salumi

This list does not pretend to include all of the cured meats of Italy. Instead, you will find some of the more popular and well-known types that you might encounter when traveling, along with a smattering of some interesting traditional varieties. The respective regions are listed in parentheses.

Northern Italy

bresaola: beef (sometimes deer) thigh or loin (Lombardy)
bresaola della Valdossola: veal thigh or loin (Piemonte)
bresaola di cavallo: horse (Lombardy, Veneto)
coppa: pork neck (Emilia-Romagna)
cotechino: beef and poultry sausage (Piemonte)
cotechino: pork sausage (Emilia-Romagna)
cotechino: pork sausage (Friuli-Venezia Giulia)
cotechino alla vaniglia: pork sausage with vanilla (Lombardy)
cotechino cremonese "vaniglia": sweet pork sausage (Emilia-Romagna)
culatello: pork rump (Emilia-Romagna)
fiocchetto: pork thigh (Emilia-Romagna)
lardo al rosmarino di Cavour: pork fat in rosemary (Piemonte)
lardo di Arnad DOP: pork fat (Val d'Aosta)
mocetta (motzetta): goat thigh (Val d'Aosta)
pancetta piacentina DOP: rolled pork belly (Emilia-Romagna)
pancetta steccata: flattened pork belly (Emilia-Romagna)
petto d'oca: goose breast (Lombardy)
prosciutto crudo d'oca: goose leg (Friuli-Venezia Giulia)
prosciutto di Parma: pork ham (Emilia-Romagna)
prosciutto di San Daniele: pork ham (Friuli-Venezia Giulia)
salame d'asino: donkey (sometimes beef) thigh or shoulder and pork pancetta salame (Piemonte, Veneto)
salame da sugo: pork liver and tongue salame (Emilia-Romagna)
salame di Felino: pork salame (Emilia-Romagna)
salame di patate: potato and pork salame (Piemonte)
salame di Varzi DOP: pork salame (Lombardy)
salame d'oca: goose salame
salame d'oca di Mortara IGP: goose salame (Friuli-Venezia Giulia, Lombardy)
salame gentile: pork salame (Emilia-Romagna)
salame milano (crespone): pork and beef salame (Lombardy)
speck: smoked boned pork ham (Trentino Alto Adige)
zampone di Modena IGP: stuffed pork trotter (several regions)

Central Italy

ciauscolo (ciavuscolo, ciabuscolo): pork sausage (Marches)
finocchiona (sbriciolona): pork salame with fennel seeds (Tuscany)
lonza: pork neck (Marche, Tuscany)
mazzafegati: pork and liver sausage (Umbria, Marches)
rigatino: pork belly (Tuscany)
salame di cinghiale: wild boar salame (Tuscany)
salame toscano: pork salame (Tuscany)
salsiccia di cinghiale: wild boar sausage (Tuscany)
soppressata: cooked pork head, skin, and tongue sausage (Tuscany)
tarese Valdarno: pork belly (Tuscany)

Southern Italy

capocollo: pork neck (several regions)
guanciale amatriciano: pork cheeks or jaw (Abruzzo, Lazio)
lucania: pork sausage (Basilicata)
mortadella di Amatrice: pork salame (Lazio)
mortadella di Campotosto: pork salame with a strip of lardo (Abruzzo, Lazio)
pancetta arrotolata dei Monti Nebrodi: pork belly (Sicily)
salame di Napoli: pork salame (Campania)
salsiccia di fegato (fegatazzo): pork liver, heart, and lung sausage (sometimes also sweetbreads, belly, and cheeks) (Abruzzo, Molise)
soppressata (sopprassata, sopressa): pork salame (Campania, Molise, Puglia)
vescica: pork bladder filled with sausage and soppressata (Basilicata)

Salting and Additives

Aging meat without treatment causes it to turn an unattractive gray color. Now, as in ancient times, dry salt or a brine solution is blended in with the meat mixture to avoid this discoloration. According to Harold McGee in *On Food and Cooking,* scientists have discovered that in the past it was actually an impurity in the salt, a nitrate that, on reacting with the bacteria on the meat, evolved into nitrite, which reacted with the pig-ment in the muscle to keep the meat pink. Sodium ni-trite is a simple salt ($NaNO_2$) now used industrially for the same purpose. It is valued for its efficiency in maintain-ing color, for its ability to retard oxidation (rancidity) in fat, and its efficacy in inhibiting bacteria, especially those that cause botulism. Ascorbic acid is sometimes added to speed up the curing process and boost color and flavor.

Another occasional additive in salame is pow-dered milk, used because it amalgamates the mix-ture, absorbs extra humidity, and keeps the mixture soft. The use of salts, nitrites, and ascorbic acid were absolutely essential in the days of no refrigeration. With the advent of the modern conveniences of coolers and freezers, the levels of nitrites and nitrates have been reduced substantially.

Drying and Aging

Once the meat has been salted, it must undergo a drying process at relatively warm temperatures. This causes the moisture released by the salt to be expelled and evaporated. Once the moisture has been elimi-nated, the extended drying process at ambient tem-peratures can begin. The length of aging is dependent on climate and the size of the product being aged.

Mold is an important effect of the aging process. As it develops on the sur-face of the meat, it regulates humidity, allowing the prod-uct to dry slowly and uni-formly. In the first three or four days, white mold grows only near the lean parts. After two or three months, the skin is uniformly covered in white or gray to green mold. The amino acids and peptides in the meat react with beneficial molds to neutralize any nonbeneficial molds. Controlling the temperature and humidity helps to avoid the produc-tion of toxic molds; the ideal conditions are tempera-tures under 20°C (70°F), with a relative humidity lower than 80 percent.

Smoking

Smoking is essentially cooking at a very low temper-ature. According to Harold McGee, wood smoke can contain as many as two hundred components, such as alcohols, acids, phenol compounds, and some toxic substances. These substances inhibit the growth of bacteria and retard fat oxidation. And best of all, the smoky flavor of burning wood is infused in the meat. Hot smoking fully cooks the meat in a relatively short time, with a temperature above 145°F. Cold smoking is done over longer periods at a temperature of less than 100°F. Smoking is used in regions where the climate isn't conducive to drying, such as in the south of Italy, where it is hot and humid, or in the north, where it is very cold.

Cooking

Cooked *salume* should also be mentioned. Mortadella, a cooked salame, may be the most recognized Italian cured meat in America, and it is just as popular in Italy.

Highly processed and highly industrialized, it is practically a household word. In recent years, the Italian product has been allowed to be imported to the United States. The demand in Italy and abroad is now so high that it can only be met by high-production industry. Mortadella is found in several regions of Italy, with a wide range of variations.

After all of the prime cuts of pork have been used, the last product made is usually the sausage prepared with the leftover parts. These pieces are chopped and stuffed into a casing or skin and cooked, or cooked first and then shaped

An interesting example of the curing process is seen in a product called lardo. The name of this divine cured fat is unfortunately similar to the English word *lard*. Lard is rendered, often from low-quality fat. Lardo is a cured high-quality fat from the pork back or jaw. The back results in a slab, and the jaw is a cylinder shape.

Several regions produce a version of lardo. In Tuscany, lardo di Colonnata has earned high acclaim due to the process of maturing it in marble containers (see page 14). Ten years ago, there were two producers. With the fame of the product came a growth in the number of producers. Today, fourteen producers of lardo di Colonnata can provide 220,000 pounds a year. It sounds like a lot, especially considering the miniscule size of the village with its three hundred inhabitants. But it is very little compared to the nearly 20 million pounds made by industrial producers. With fame came competition and imitations. The artisanal producers have worked hard to keep the character and true tradition of this product, to the point that it has now received IGP status (see page 30). The boundaries have been carefully defined to just a few hectares surrounding Colonnata, in recognition of its unique microclimate.

lardo di Colonnata
Tuscany

The remote village of Colonnata is near the marble quarries in the rugged mountains sixteen hundred feet above Carrara. At one end of the piazza are the remnants of Roman marble columns. Near the church stands a statue of St. Bartholomew, the patron saint of butchers. There is a haunting sense of stepping back in time in this village. It's easy to imagine how difficult life must have been in the past in this remote area. It doesn't look as if much has changed in the surroundings since Michelangelo came to choose the marble for his sculptures. The quarry workers lived off of the land then and prepared a product, lardo di Colonnata, which was destined to fame, but not for another five hundred years.

Lardo di Colonnata is a cured high-quality pork fat that comes from the right and left of the pig's spine; the fat is pure white until it reaches near the belly, where it takes on some pink striations. It is seasoned with aromatics and left to age in a conca, a marble container. In its humble beginnings, lardo was considered peasant food and was the perfect lunch to carry up the mountains to work, for it was full of calories to sustain the men through their day. Contrary to other areas, where fatty meats are eaten to keep people warm in the winter, in Colonnata, lean meats were eaten in the winter, and the energy-providing lardo would be saved for the period of heavy work.

The modern polished gray-veined white marble containers for lardo production stand about three feet high. The older ones and those for home use are smaller, rough, and chiseled. They are cleaned well, then rubbed with fresh garlic. The two-inch-high slabs of fat are rubbed with salt, then layered with each producer's secret combination of spices and herbs. The base mixture is sea salt, rosemary, garlic, and ground pepper. Other spices may be added, such as cinnamon, cloves, fennel seed, star anise, oregano, sage, juniper berries, and cardamom. After the containers are filled, they are covered and the fat is left to cure in cool, humid underground cellars. The marble boxes with their covers look a bit like tombs.

Colonnata is high enough to stay relatively cool in the summers, and the marble containers maintain the temperature well. After at least six months of aging, or up to ten, the lardo is ready to slice. The rind is removed, and the thin white and pink slices look like cold, clean marble. The lardo from Colonnata is fragrant with herbal aromas, with a sweet and buttery taste. It is delicious simply draped over a piece of fresh bread or wrapped around ripe melon. Sometimes, a spread for crostini is made with lardo finely chopped with garlic, scallions, salt, and herbs. Or try the quarry worker's sandwich, made with thick slices of lardo, tomato, and raw onion.

culatello di Zibello
Emilia-Romagna

From those lucky enough to have tasted culatello di Zibello, cured pork rump produced near Parma, there may be a collective sigh of relief for a product that was nearly lost. Through intense lobbying by some of the producers, the consortium for culatello di Zibello came about in October 1996, when the zone was finally granted DOP standing. Leading the initiative was Massimo Spigaroli, president of the consortium. Spigaroli and the other eleven producers from the area subject themselves to strict regulations regarding the traditional process of handling and curing the meat and its origins and treatment prior to butchering. Rather than following the new rules set forth by the European Union (which include white-tiled and temperature-controlled rooms), the antique discipline has been allowed to follow its traditional technique of aging the meat in musky, dark rooms.

Instead of using the whole leg to make prosciutto, just the rump is cut, seasoned, and hand-tied in a bladder. What makes culatello so special is the high quality of the pig breeds, the hands-on method of preparation, and the foggy climate of the tiny pocket of Emilia-Romagna where it is made. Culatello can only be produced in a small area called the Bassa Parmense. The zone, which is less than seventy-five square miles, is bordered on the north by the Po River and stretches south to the tangent rivers Taro and Ongina. Eight communities are permitted to make the handmade product that is legally named culatello di Zibello: Busseto, Polesine Parmenese, San Secondo, Zibello, Soragna, Colorno, Roccabianca, and Sissa. The first registered trademark was in Zibello, and the name stuck when the Denominazione di Origine Protetta (DOP), the protection of the area of production, was defined to include the other areas.

Culatello di Zibello received a lot of attention when it achieved DOP status. As a result, industrial producers began to make another product also called culatello. It looks the same, but is made year-round by artificially creating the humidity and temperature controls. Most of the work is done under refrigeration in rooms lined with ceramic tiles. The law for the industrial products allows the use of chemical additives. You can always identify the true artisan product, because it will have the trademark and be called Culatello di Zibello.

CULATELLO
DI ZIBELLO

zona di
produzione

The Italian consortium for

culatello di Zibello

inspects culatello after

eleven months of aging.

If it passes the inspection,

it receives the trademark

for culatello di Zibello.

prosciutto

Several regions have a version of prosciutto, the cured hind legs of pork and other meats. The most famous, and most exported, of the cured pork legs known as prosciutto crudo (cured raw pork) are the branded hams from Parma, in the region of Emilia-Romagna and from San Daniele in the region of Friuli-Venezia Giulia. Each has a unique microclimate and methodology, and both result in a delicate, sweet product.

Prosciutto di Parma is a perfect example of a product that has been industrialized, yet maintains its quality and traditional flavor. All aspects of manufacture, from the breeding of the pigs and their care to the packaging of the end product, are rigidly controlled by the Istituto Parma Qualità (IPQ). The yearly quota of eight million *prosciutti* comes from 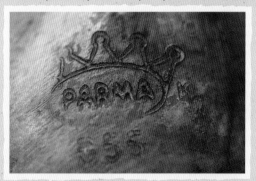 just over two hundred producers. The source of these *prosciutti* is four million pigs, most from a breed called Large White, which originated in England in the late 1700s. A cross between a Chinese pig and an English pig, this tasty animal weighs in at over three hundred pounds. It appeared in the Bourbon court in Naples in the early nineteenth century. They are raised on some six thousand pig farms near Parma. A consortium-approved prosciutto will have the trademark PARMA inside a crown branded on it.

In the farthest northeast corner of Italy, between the Alps and the sea, is the region of Friuli. While prosciutto di San Daniele uses the same breeds of pigs as Parma, the production method varies a bit. Each thigh of a minimum weight of eleven kilograms is flattened and given a violin shape, with the hoof still intact. The aging process includes the step of covering the ham in a paste of lard and cereal to keep it from drying too quickly. The results are a moister texture and a rosy pink color, with a sweet aftertaste. The zone of production is smaller than that of Parma, with fewer than thirty producers yielding a total of 1.7 million hams per year. The consortium for San Daniele places a brand in the shape of a leg with the letters SD in the center, surrounded by the words *prosciutto di San Daniele*. From the same region comes speck, a lightly smoked boneless ham.

A currently popular food on menus in Italy, prosciutto crudo d'oca, is made with the leg of goose. It was historically created for the Jewish population in Friuli-Venezia Giulia as an alternative to prosciutto di San Daniele, also from the area. The leg is boned and cured in coarse sea salt, pepper, nutmeg, and bay leaves for six weeks. It is then coated with pepper and dried in an airy space for at least two or up to five months. Other regions also make prosciutto from goose, such as Lombardy, where the leg is first marinated in Marsala, then seasoned with salt, pepper, nutmeg, and bay leaves for forty to fifty days. A relatively new designation, *ecumenico* ("ecumenical"), has been given to some of the goose products by the Istituto Nazionale di Sociologia Rurale to signify that it can be consumed by three religions: Catholic, Jewish, and Muslim.

During my research for this book, I heard a joke about a farmer who had a pig with a wooden leg. Once, a traveler stopped to ask how the pig happened to have a wooden leg. The farmer explained that his pig, Beppe, was very special. "One day," he said, "my son was drowning, and Beppe saved him. He's a hero!"

"Great," said the traveler, "but how did he get a wooden leg?"

The farmer replied, "He's a very brave pig; one night our barn was on fire, and Beppe stood on his back legs and rang the doorbell to wake us up. We were able to save the barn from burning down because of him. He is a super-special pig!"

The traveler was beginning to be exasperated. "But how did he get the wooden leg?"

The farmer replied, "Well, when you have a pig that special, you don't eat him all at once!"

prosciutto di Parma

Emilia-Romagna

Each region of Italy makes a version of prosciutto, the most famous being prosciutto di Parma. The conditions for making prosciutto are most favorable south of Parma in the valley of Langhirano. The salting is done artfully, to ensure a safely cured meat that is not overly salty. In other regions, prosciutto di Parma is called *dolce,* or sweet, prosciutto.

One of the oldest producers in Langhirano is the company of Pio Tosini. Ferrante Tosini founded it in 1905, and twenty years later, his son Pio developed it into a viable business. The acorn logo represents the food that the pigs ate in the past when they roamed the hills.

Today, Ferrante's grandson Renato Ghersetich and great-grandsons Nicola Ghersetich and Giovanni Bianchi carry on the family tradition. The annual production of 100,000 *prosciutti* is considered small in comparison to that of other producers. But by keeping production small, the company has been able to maintain quality and hygiene, and as a result they are one of the few producers permitted to export to the United States. Nicola proudly says, "As in the past, the only ingredients used to make an excellent prosciutto are high-quality pork, salt, and air. The rest is up to us." The plant, one of the first built in the area, is in an ideal position for aging, at the bottom of the valley, cooled by constant breezes from the river. Every aspect of the production is controlled, from the diet and breeding of the pigs to the processing operation.

"The pigs, Large White and Duroc breeds, are not bred for lean meat, but for flavor," Ghersetich explains. "We choose first-choice meat that has been carefully bred and raised with the best type of nutrition." At the beginning of the process, each fresh ham weighs from eleven to sixteen kilos. They are first massaged with rollers to remove any remaining blood. Most of this work is done by machines, but part of it still must be done by hand, especially around the bone. The hams are then coated with salt, which penetrates the flesh as a result of the massaging. The ham then rests for five days at 1° to 4°C (34° to 36°F). It is then resalted and left in the cooler again for nineteen days. The hams are then placed in a blower to remove the salt. A blower is used because, under U.S. regulations, the traditional brushes cannot be used. At this point, the hams are moved to coolers maintained at 1° to 4°C (34° to 36°F). After sixty days, the hams are trimmed by hand, then returned to the cooler. At one hundred days, they are washed and kept at 15° to 20°C (60° to 70°F) until dried, then replaced in the cooler rooms to age for at least twelve months.

All of the curing is done in ambient air with tall floor-to-ceiling windows that are left open at night to

capture the cool river breezes. Prosciutto di Parma was the first Italian ham approved for export to the United States. The U.S. Code of Federal Regulations follows rather closely the rigid discipline already defined by the Consortium for Prosciutto di Parma. Along with the constraint on using the brushes, the only additional restriction that the U.S. regulation required was that the hams had to be aged a minimum of four hundred days, the length of time deemed necessary to eliminate any possible disease. In the past, producers aged the hams for ten months or more, but recently the consortium has decided to implement a rule of a minimum twelve months of aging before the hams are sold. The best are aged for sixteen to eighteen months, and the maximum time for aging is 2½ years. Prosciutto di Parma is one of the success stories of a traditional product that has maintained its quality, even in mass production.

Each ham is labeled with a button that shows the month and the year the ham went into production, as well as the identification codes of the butcher, slaughterhouse, and farm where the pig was raised. The finished weight is between seven and twelve kilos.

Nicola Ghersetich sent me up a road called the Via del Sale into the hills for lunch. This road is so named because it was the ancient route for bringing salt from the sea. Here, in a trattoria, I tried some of the Tosini two-year-old ham. The delicate rose-colored leaves of prosciutto were served in the classic way, simply with fresh sliced bread. Like most prosciutto, this high-quality meat is usually eaten raw, sometimes with seasonal fruit.

pancetta

Pancetta, sometimes called Italian bacon, is cured pork belly. In general, there are two versions: in one, the pancetta is cured in a slab and used as a flavoring in cooking; the other type is rolled and used as a thinly sliced cold cut for antipasti and panini. Italian-style pancetta produced outside of Italy is usually the rolled variety, and it can be used in cooking or on an antipasto platter. From region to region the name changes, but the flavor is always a pleasant combination of sweet and salty. The usual curing method is to coat it with salt or soak it in brine for a week to ten days, then rinse it with wine vinegar and reseason with salt and pepper. It is then aged for at least thirty days in a temperature- and humidity-controlled place. Some versions are also smoked.

Parma produces pancetta steccata, which is shaped and aged between two flat pieces of wood. It is a rather recent innovation, dating back to the 1960s. The technique came from the increased use of breeds of pork that were prolific but of lower quality. The rolled type of pancetta using meat from these breeds was difficult to make because the layers of fat and meat would not adhere to each other, which allowed air to enter and cause rancidity. The new technique was to fold the pancetta and sew the edges closed, then press the mass flat between two flat pieces of wood that were held tightly with an elastic cord. After twenty-four to thirty-six hours of pressing, the pancetta is left to age at least five to six months or up to two years, according to the size and the humidity.

In Tuscany, pancetta may also be called rigatino, tarese, or ventresca. The belly remains under salt for forty-eight hours and is then cleaned with a mixture made from boiled vinegar and *peperoncino* (hot red pepper). After it dries, it is coated in pepper and *peperoncino* and left to age for two to four months. Another version from San Miniato uses wild fennel seed instead of *peperoncino* and is folded and tied before aging. Tarese Valdarno, made near Florence, is a type of pancetta that is made with a cut that includes the belly up to the spine. It is rubbed with a mixture of chopped red garlic, pepper, orange zest, and juniper. After ten days under salt it is rinsed and dried, then rubbed again with the red garlic mixture, salted again, and aged for two to three months.

The southern regions produce several highly seasoned versions. A version in Martina Franca (in the Puglia region) rests in brine for twenty days, then is marinated in cooked wine for twenty-four hours. Rolled tightly, it is dried for two weeks and is then smoked, and finally it is aged from sixty to a hundred days. In Sicily, pancetta arrotolata dei Monti Nebrodi is rolled tightly and brined in a mixture of salt, wild fennel, garlic, oregano, and vinegar for fifteen days, then dried and covered with pepper, *peperoncino,* garlic, and oregano and aged for three to four months.

pancetta di Cinta Senese

Tuscany

Six years ago, I spent the good part of a year coordinating cooking courses at a little castle near Gaiole in Chianti. We purchased our meat from Vincenzo Chini, a butcher in Gaiole whom I remember most for his incredibly fresh and clean meats and also for the butcher paper he wrapped them in. I recently returned to pay him a visit.

Vincenzo and his brother, Cesare, are carrying on a family business that has existed since 1682. Chini was the first producer to be officially recognized to make *salumi* from the Cinta Senese pig. Vincenzo's son raises the pigs nearby at his farm, Montechioccioli, much as his ancestors did. He started with some of the best examples of the animals he could find and has since carefully selected them to perfect the breed. According to the Chini family, "The best *salumi* are born from good breeding and care."

The Cinta Senese breed has been raised in the province of Siena since medieval times. A quasi-feral pig, it was abandoned to near-extinction in the 1950s, when it was replaced by faster-growing, leaner domestic breeds. Just in time, it has been rediscovered. Even though it has a higher percentage of fat, it is a high-quality fat, and the meat is dense and full of flavor (it's the fat that gives pork its flavor). This breed of pig is easy to recognize by its markings: a black head and body, except for a white "belt" that circles the front of the body, including the two front legs (*cinta* means "belt," and *senese* means "of Siena").

Since 2000, the breed has been protected by a consortium that oversees the husbandry, feed, and production of *salumi* and meats. The breeders are required to allow the pigs to live as they did traditionally: outdoors grazing in woods and meadows on a diet of roots, tubers, acorns, and other foraged plants. Much attention is paid to the health and well-being of the animals. The meat products are identified with codes for the breeder, the pig, the year of butchering, and the number of each piece produced.

Before I left, Vincenzo had me taste his melt-in-the-mouth pancetta. "The pancetta of the Cinta Senese is particularly good because the fat has so much flavor," he explained. He leaves it one week under fine salt, then rinses it with water. It is dipped in vinegar, coated in pepper, then hung to age for thirty days. While pancetta is often used in cooking, this exquisite product is best sliced thin and served on a platter with an assortment of prosciutto and salame.

While visiting Vincenzo Chini, he recounted a story about a special pig named Pippo raised by his family: "When he was born, his mother rolled over him and squashed him. This happens a lot with pigs, because the mothers are so large and the babies are so small. We took him to the vet and asked if there was any hope. The vet said that as long as he was breathing there was hope. So we took him home. We had to feed him with an eyedropper, and we kept him in the house. He got better, and we started feeding him soft food. Pretty soon we made a bed for him in the corner of the room. After that, he began to walk, and he followed us everywhere like a puppy. He is six years old now and weighs three hundred kilos."

salame and sausages

Until refrigeration became available, most butchering was traditionally done in the winter. The leaner meat pieces (leg and shoulder, for example) and other large cuts would be left to cure, while the smaller, second-quality pieces were chopped and made into *salami*. The trimming of the lean meats yielded small pieces of high-quality meat that were usually finely chopped and blended with some fat, seasoned, and put in casings to make fresh sausages. These classic Tuscan sausages are seasoned simply with salt, pepper, and some garlic, and they are delicious grilled or cooked in stews.

Another popular sausage is the luganega (lucanica). Though found in the north, it originally came from the southern region of Basilicata. It is usually made with shoulder and prime cuts of the neck, with the tendons and fat removed. The meat is ground with salt, pepper, fennel seeds, and a little ground *peperoncino,* then is put into lamb casings and left to rest in wicker baskets overnight. The next morning, it is hung to dry for fifteen to twenty days in a dry, drafty attic. In the beginning, a fireplace is always lit. The traditional shape is called quattro gambi, or "four legs," and is shaped like a W, whereas the luganega from Lombardy in the north is sometimes called salsiccia a metro, "sausage by the meter," because it is sold by the meter.

soppressata di Gioi
Campania

Only three families make a unique salame called soppressata di Gioi, which is a dense, lean salame kept moist with a thread of lardo running down the center. A salame prepared this way is called lardellato and is usually found in Abruzzo. Soppressata di Gioi is the only salame lardellato in Campania. There are probably not more than ten families in the village of Gioi, which is fifty kilometers east of Agropoli in southern Campania.

One of the families, Raffaele Barbato and his wife, Giuliana Nese, butcher about fifty of their own pigs a year. From each pig they can get thirty-five to forty salami. They also make sausages, capocollo, and pancetta. The breeds are mixed, coming from the mountains

locally. Their feed is organic, primarily grown on the farm: squash, beets, acorns, chestnuts, grains, corn, and other seasonal products.

"The work is best done in the cool months, from October to April," says Barbato. The meat, only from the leg, is coarsely chopped by hand, mixed with salt and pepper (some of the other producers use *peperoncino* and/or fennel seed), and left to rest for about ten hours.

Meanwhile, the fat is cut into long, thin strips and left buried under salt for at least three to four hours.

The meat is put into natural casings, and the strip of lardo is carefully worked into the center, packing the filling into the casing tightly and shaping it at the same time.

The *salami* rest on a table for twelve hours, then are turned to rest for another twelve hours. At this point, they are hung to dry in a room with a wood fire burning constantly for at least thirty days. The lardo keeps the meat from drying out too quickly. The *salami* are cleaned every few days and brushed with olive oil. When they are finished aging, if they are not to be consumed at once, they are stored under lard or olive oil or are vacuum packed.

sausages and salami
Tuscany

Forty kilometers south of Siena is Belsedere, an organic farm that encompasses a thousand acres. In addition to producing wheat, pecorino cheese, and extra-virgin olive oil, the owners produce typical *salumi* made from their own stock of pigs.

I first met Contessa Ada Avanzati in 1996, when I came to Belsedere to see her organic production of pecorino cheese. It was the beginning of a lovely friendship for me.

In 1963, intent on keeping her ancestral farm intact, the Contessa began producing *salumi* and pecorino cheese." Today, her son, Venceslao de Gori Pannilini; his wife, Silvia Paoletti; and their two children, Niccolò and Federica, carry on the work.

Butchers Marino Menchetti and Mauro Mencarelli have worked at Belsedere for more than fifteen years. The pigs are raised on the farm and are butchered on Friday, cut into parts, and left to age in coolers over the weekend. On Monday, the pancetta and *prosciutti* are prepared. Fresh sausage is made on Tuesday, and Wednesday is for *salami*. You can see by the diverse shapes and sizes that this is work done by hand.

Their fresh sausages are 50 percent fat and 50 percent coarsely ground lean pork and are seasoned only with salt, pepper, and some garlic. The ingredients are put into a large mixer that amalgamates them well. The sterilized natural casings are purchased commercially and come in a dried, salted form. They are left to soften in a mixture of vinegar and water. They fit directly onto a nozzle from which the meat is extruded. The butchers tie the sausages at four-inch lengths and pierce the skin to allow the air to release. The sausages are ready to consume at this point, but are often left to dry in a refrigerator for a week to ten days.

The process for salame starts in a similar way. The differences are that the casings are larger, and the *salami* will dry and age much longer than the sausages. Belsedere's typical Tuscan salame is made with finely ground lean pork and 20 percent fat. In addition to salt, the seasoning also contains ground and whole pepper, garlic, a bit of sugar, and powdered milk to absorb some of the extra moisture.

Once the seasoned mixture is ready, it is stuffed into veal casings and left in a warm room (20°C). After a day or two, the temperature is lowered to 15°C (60°F) for another five to six days; then the *salami* are ready to age. The *salami* are aged from one to two months, depending on the size. When sliced, the meat is fragrant and tender yet hearty, perfect to serve with the Contessa's pecorino cheese.

Now, at the age of ninety-four, the Contessa has officially retired. She spends her days resting in the sun and visiting her chapel and leaves the rest of the work to her capable family.

regulations

Traditional and Industrial Products

Food products come and go for many reasons, including trends and the scarcity of ingredients. In the last twenty years, cured-meat production methods have changed due to new governmental demands for strict sanitation. This is understandable, especially with regard to raw cured meats, yet it is true that people have been eating meat products cured by traditional means for centuries without harm. Generic rules and regulations can sometimes force a tiny artisanal producer out of business because he can't afford to refurbish his curing room. An artisan product forced to follow strict sanitation laws, in spite of generations of success without them, may take on a different character, causing us to lose a traditional product. A perfect example is culatello di Zibello, an artisan product that was suddenly near extinction because new European Union sanitation laws required white-tiled rooms and refrigeration for its production.

Since its creation, the European Union has been working on a set of rules and regulations for traditional foods from the member countries. It has classified each product with one of two designations, DOP or IGP. Denominazione di Origine Protetta (DOP), or Denomination of Protected Origin, specifies materials, method of production, and the zone of origin. Indicazioni Geografiche Protette (IGP), or Protected Geographic Indication, is a more general category that requires only a geographical area of origin. Depending on the product, this can be helpful, because it may protect foods from extinction. But in some cases, the definition of products that should be artisanal has been overgeneralized. This vagueness has allowed industrial producers to create a facsimile that doesn't truly replicate the traditional product.

In my travels, I have met some producers who are carrying on artisanal traditions. Included in this book are stories of some of the people who have bridged the gap between an artisan tradition and some version of commercial success without sacrificing quality.

Along with legal definitions come politics. Large industry is often better at persuading officials about a product than a handful of artisan producers. Some artisan products have found success only to be overwhelmed by industrial copies; culatello di Zibello and lardo di Colonnata are good examples. Sometimes, due to demand, industry replaces the traditional practices, and the artisan product completely disappears.

Private organizations are playing a part in protecting the artisanal products. Slow Food is an international organization that was founded by Italian Carlo Petrini in 1986. The goal of the movement, now eighty thousand members strong, is to "protect the pleasures of the table from the homogenization of modern fast food and life." One of their projects is to preserve agricultural biodiversity and traditional foods that are at risk of disappearing.

Import/Export

Of the several hundred different *salumi* available in Italy, only a handful are found in the United States. The USDA does not recognize mainland Italy as free from swine vesicular disease (SVD); classical swine fever (CSF); or bovine spongiform encephalopathy (BSE), also known as mad cow disease. The products that are allowed into the United States have been produced in

USDA-sanctioned facilities, following specific guidelines set forth by the Code of Federal Regulations. Since prior to 2003, these regulations, along with other specifications regarding temperature and environment, require dry-cured pork to be aged a minimum of four hundred days. This is the length of time deemed necessary to eliminate any possible animal disease.

In 2003, the Italian Ministry of Health (with USDA agreement) amended the official Italian government export certificate for meat products to include a new category of dry-cured pork products aged less than four hundred days. The certificate sets strict conditions for exporting these products, including a dedicated production facility that uses only raw material imported from countries recognized by the USDA as free from animal disease, as well as the requirement of deboning prior to processing.

At the time of this writing, only a few of Italy's cured-meat treasures have begun trickling into the United States. Prosciutto is permitted from approved facilities under the trademark names of prosciutto di Parma (from the region of Emilia-Romagna) and prosciutto di San Daniele (from the region of Friuli-Venezia Giulia). Some other generic Italian *prosciutti* may also be allowed from USDA-approved facilities, which means that producers in Tuscany and Umbria, for example, might also export if their facilities are approved, but for the most part these *prosciutti*

are coming from Emilia-Romagna and the northern regions. A few kinds of salame are also allowed with the same restrictions.

◆

The following recipes give some examples of how to use cured meats in cooking. Some cured meats, like pancetta, add a wonderful flavor to recipes. Many, such as prosciutto, bresaola, and cured loin, are best eaten raw; their delicate flavor and texture are lost when cooked. The classic preparation is a platter of sliced assorted meats served with fresh bread. These meats also work well added as a garnish on top of a dish or stirred in at the end of cooking.

When buying cured meats, ask the butcher to slice only what you will use in the next few days. Keep it wrapped airtight. Exposure to air will cause the meat to turn brown and rancid. Unless your butcher sells a high volume of meats, the end piece may be dark. Ask him to discard it before weighing your purchase. In general, the greater the diameter of the piece of meat, the thinner it should be sliced. Keep the slices wrapped tightly in plastic wrap to protect them from moisture loss and oxidation.

Avoid vacuum-packed salami, as the heady pungent aromas are squelched without air. Look for salami with a crinkled surface, which indicates the use of natural casings. If you buy the type with cellulose casings, remove the casing before eating. *Buon appetito!*

In Tuscany, many dinners begin with an appetizer of thinly sliced meats (affetatti) and a glass of wine. The assortment can include pancetta, lardo, and a variety of salame and cheeses, as desired. In the fall, substitute figs or pears for the sweet melon.

classic affetatti

Affetatti is Italian for sliced and is the name

for a platter of assorted _salumi_. It is sometimes accompanied

with seasonal fruit and local cheeses as well.

1 ripe cantaloupe or honeydew, peeled,
seeded, and sliced into 12 wedges

6 thin slices pancetta

6 thin slices prosciutto di Parma

12 slices finocchiona salame
(Tuscan-style salame with fennel seeds)
or your favorite salame

4 ounces mortadella, cubed

12 slices pecorino cheese

Small loaf of country bread, sliced,
or grissini (bread sticks)

Wrap each melon slice with a slice of pancetta or
prosciutto. Arrange the salame, mortadella, and cheese
on one half of a serving platter. Arrange the wrapped
melon slices on the other half of the platter. Accompany
with a basket of the sliced bread. _Serves 4_

mozzarella, tomato, and salame stacks

This is an elegant summer antipasto.

It should be assembled at the last minute.

8 ounces fresh mozzarella cheese
(2-inch-diameter balls or a braid)

8 slices salame

1 cup shredded red-leaf lettuce

8 cherry tomatoes

8 small basil leaves

Extra-virgin olive oil for drizzling

Salt and freshly ground black pepper to taste

Slice the mozzarella into 8 slices, each ½ inch thick. Place the cheese on a paper towel to drain for 10 minutes. Put a mozzarella slice on top of each slice of salame.

Place one-fourth of the lettuce on each plate. Top with 2 mozzarella-salame stacks. Split the cherry tomatoes, not quite cutting all the way through. Stick the basil leaf in the slit and place 1 tomato on top of each stack. Drizzle with olive oil, season with salt and pepper, and serve at once. *Serves 4*

gnocco fritto

This sublimely simple appetizer is from the kitchen of Laura Galli at Hosteria Giusti in Modena.

Thinly sliced prosciutto, pancetta, or culatello is placed on top of these

deep-fried pieces of dough while they are still warm; they will practically melt in your mouth.

*½ ounce (10 grams) cake yeast
(or 2 teaspoons dry yeast)*

¼ cup warm water (105° to 115°F)

1 cup unbleached all-purpose flour

*2 tablespoons unsalted butter
at room temperature*

About 1 teaspoon carbonated mineral water

Olive oil for deep-frying

*12 slices prosciutto di Parma, pancetta,
and/or culatello*

In a small bowl, combine the yeast and the warm water and stir until the yeast is dissolved. Let stand until foamy, about 10 minutes.

Mound the flour on a work surface and make a well in the center. Add the yeast mixture, butter, and enough mineral water to produce a soft dough. Knead until smooth.

Put the dough in a medium bowl and cut an X on top. Cover and let rise for at least 20 minutes or up to 1 hour, or until the dough has doubled.

Transfer the dough to a lightly floured work surface. Roll the dough out to a ¼-inch thickness. With a ravioli cutter or knife, cut the dough into 12 2-inch-wide diamonds.

In a large, heavy saucepan, heat 3 inches of oil over medium-high heat until hot, but not smoking. Add the dough pieces a few at a time. Fry, turning once, for about 2 minutes on each side, until golden brown. Using a wire skimmer, transfer to paper towels to drain. Place in a low oven to keep warm while frying the remaining pieces. Place the gnocco on a platter, drape with the desired meats, and serve warm. *Makes 12*

asparagus wrapped with bresaola

For this delicious antipasto, you can also substitute prosciutto for the bresaola. Make ahead and chill, or serve warm, drizzled with a little extra-virgin olive oil and balsamic vinegar.

18 spears asparagus (about 8 ounces), trimmed

6 paper-thin slices bresaola, chilled

Peel the bottom 2 to 3 inches of each asparagus spear lightly with a vegetable peeler.

In a large pot of salted boiling water, blanch the asparagus for 3 to 5 minutes, or until crisp-tender. Drain and immediately immerse in ice water for 3 to 5 minutes, just to stop the cooking. When cool, drain and pat dry.

With a very sharp knife, cut the chilled bresaola into 1-inch-wide strips.

Wrap a meat strip around the middle of each asparagus spear. Arrange on a tray for passing.

Serves 6

fricò with potatoes and pancetta

This cheese pancake comes from Friuli in northeast Italy. Several variations are found there: some pancakes are soft, some are crunchy, and some are made with polenta or just cheese.

2 tablespoons extra-virgin olive oil

4 ounces smoked pancetta, diced

1 onion, thinly sliced

2 large potatoes (about 1 pound), peeled and shredded

2 cups water

Salt and freshly ground black pepper to taste

6 ounces Montasio or Parmigiano-Reggiano cheese, grated

In a medium, heavy sauté pan, heat the olive oil over medium-high heat. Add the pancetta and onion and cook for 4 to 5 minutes, or until golden brown. Add the potatoes, water, and salt and pepper. Decrease the heat to medium, cover, and simmer for 30 minutes, or until the potatoes are tender. Add the cheese and stir until melted.

Place a medium nonstick sauté pan over medium-high heat. Transfer the cheese mixture to the heated pan. Spread the mixture out evenly. Cook for 5 to 6 minutes to form a golden crust. Slide the pancake onto a plate and invert it back into the pan. Brown on the second side for 4 to 6 minutes. Cut into quarters and serve warm. *Serves 8*

prosciutto and stracchino pinwheels

Ask your butcher to slice the prosciutto a little thicker than usual. These pinwheels are best made ahead of time and refrigerated before serving. If you can't find stracchino, substitute another fresh soft cheese, such as mascarpone.

16 slices prosciutto di Parma, chilled

3 ounces stracchino cheese

1 cup arugula leaves

Lay the prosciutto out on a work surface. Spread with a thin layer of stracchino, then a single layer of arugula leaves. Roll lengthwise, cut into 2-inch lengths, and place on a platter. Refrigerate until ready to serve. *Serves 4*

three types of crostini

Crostini are delicious little savory toasts with toppings, designed to stimulate the appetite.

Here are three different spreads that can be made ahead to top toasts at the last moment.

Prosciutto Purée

3 ounces prosciutto di Parma

1 tablespoon extra-virgin olive oil

6 oil-cured black olives, halved and pitted

Chopped Bresaola

3 ounces bresaola, finely chopped

1 tablespoon extra-virgin olive oil

1 small Red Delicious apple, finely diced

Julienned Salame

1 small red bell pepper, roasted, peeled, and cut into julienne (see page 107)

3 ounces spicy salame, cut into julienne

9 slices country-style bread, lightly toasted and halved

To make the prosciutto topping: In a food processor, combine the prosciutto and olive oil. Process until smooth. Stir in the olives by hand.

To make the bresaola topping: In a bowl, combine all the ingredients and stir well.

To make the salame topping: In a bowl, combine the bell pepper and salame and stir well.

Spread or spoon a small amount of each topping onto 6 half-slices of the toasted bread. Arrange on a platter and serve at once. *Serves 6*

grilled prawns and zucchini wrapped with pancetta

Instead of skewers, try using stripped stems of rosemary branches. The length of the stem will determine the number of shrimp you can put on. It is easier to thread the ingredients onto the rosemary if you pierce them first with a bamboo skewer.

16 prawns or large shrimp

8 thin slices pancetta, halved

4 baby zucchini or 2 medium zucchini, cut crosswise into ½-inch-thick slices

Olive oil for brushing

Salt and freshly ground black pepper to taste

Prepare a hot fire in a charcoal grill or preheat a gas grill to medium-high. Soak 4 wooden skewers in water for 30 minutes.

Shell and devein the prawns, leaving the head (if attached) and tail intact.

Wrap each prawn with half of a slice of pancetta. Thread 4 prawns crosswise onto each of the 4 skewers, alternating with zucchini slices. Brush with oil and season with salt and pepper. Place the skewers on the grill rack and grill, turning once, for about 2 minutes on each side, until the shrimp are pink and firm. Serve at once. *Serves 4*

panini

ciabatta with salame, artichokes, and rosemary

Ciabatta, which means "slipper," is a flat, wide loaf of bread that is good to use for making sandwiches. The marinated artichokes add a little tartness to this classic sandwich. If you want to give it more pizzazz, add some marinated spicy peppers.

1 loaf ciabatta bread

12 slices salame

*6 oil-packed sun-dried tomatoes,
drained and cut into julienne*

*6 marinated baby artichokes or artichoke hearts,
drained and thinly sliced*

1 teaspoon minced fresh rosemary

Extra-virgin olive oil for drizzling

Salt and freshly ground black pepper to taste

Using a large bread knife, slice the ciabatta in half lengthwise. On the bottom half, arrange the salame and sprinkle with the sun-dried tomatoes and artichokes. Season with the rosemary, drizzle with olive oil, and sprinkle with salt and pepper. Top with the remaining ciabatta half and cut into crosswise slices to serve. *Serves 4*

open-faced sandwiches with bresaola, Gorgonzola, and radicchio

These sandwiches combine three intense flavors.

Great with ice cold Italian beer on a picnic.

*8 ounces Gorgonzola dolce latte cheese
at room temperature*

*4 large slices country-style bread,
lightly toasted*

8 slices bresaola

*Leaves from 1 small head radicchio,
cut into julienne*

Extra-virgin olive oil for drizzling

In a bowl, mash the Gorgonzola with a wooden spoon until it is spreadable. Spread evenly on the bread. Top each sandwich with 2 slices of bresaola and a pinch of radicchio. Drizzle with olive oil and serve. *Serves 4*

tramezzini of crispy pancetta, tomato, and lettuce

Tramezzini are small triangular tea sandwiches found

in Italian coffee bars. They are made with a variety of fillings,

ranging from tuna salad to ham and cheese.

12 slices pancetta

Mayonnaise for spreading

8 thin slices white or
whole-wheat sandwich bread

4 lettuce leaves

1 tomato, thinly sliced

2 hard-cooked eggs, sliced

Heat a large, heavy sauté pan over medium-high heat. Add the pancetta and fry, turning once, for about 3 minutes on each side, or until crisp. Using tongs, transfer to paper towels to drain.

Spread the mayonnaise on the bread and assemble 4 sandwiches, each with thin layers of lettuce, tomato, pancetta, and egg. Cut each sandwich in half diagonally to form 2 triangles. Serve at once. *Serves 4*

goat cheese, salame, and olive panini

Choose a salame that is sweet and won't overpower the subtleness of the goat cheese.

3 ounces salame, thinly sliced

½ cup oil-cured black olives, pitted and coarsely chopped

12 cherry tomatoes, halved

2 tablespoons red wine vinegar

2 tablespoons extra-virgin olive oil

Salt and freshly ground black pepper to taste

4 ounces fresh goat cheese at room temperature

8 slices country-style bread

4 red lettuce leaves

In a small bowl, combine the salame, olives, and tomatoes. Drizzle with the vinegar and olive oil. Season with salt and pepper and mix well.

Spread the goat cheese on each slice of bread. Assemble the sandwiches with the salame mixture and a lettuce leaf and serve at once. *Serves 4*

toasted focaccia
with coppa and provolone

Italians love this simple but flavorful sandwich made with the thin slices of meat and cheese.

*4 pieces focaccia (each about 4 inches square),
sliced in half horizontally*

Extra-virgin olive oil for brushing

8 thin slices coppa or salame of choice

8 slices provolone cheese

Brush the cut sides of the focaccia lightly with olive oil. Place one-half of each focaccia on a work surface and top each with 2 slices of coppa and 2 slices of provolone. Toast cheese side up under a broiler, on a grill, or in a toaster oven until the cheese is slightly melted. Top with the other piece of focaccia and serve at once. *Serves 4*

piadina with prosciutto and arugula

Many cultures have a griddled flatbread, and Italy is no exception. Piadina is a flatbread found in the eastern part of Emilia-Romagna and is the perfect vehicle for the region's delectable cured meats.

2 cups unbleached all-purpose flour

½ teaspoon salt

½ teaspoon baking soda

3 tablespoons cold unsalted butter

About ½ cup warm water

Olive oil for brushing

8 thin slices prosciutto di Parma

1 cup coarsely chopped arugula

In a large bowl, combine the flour, salt, and baking soda. Using a pastry cutter or 2 dinner knives, cut in the butter until it looks like coarse meal. Gradually stir in enough warm water to bring the dough together. Transfer to a lightly floured work surface and knead until smooth and not sticky.

Divide the dough into 8 equal pieces and roll the dough into 6-inch rounds, each about ⅛ inch thick.

Heat a heavy skillet over medium-high heat and brush lightly with olive oil. Cook the dough rounds, turning once, for about 1 minute on each side, or until lightly browned.

While still warm, top each bread round with 2 slices of prosciutto and a pinch of arugula. Fold in half and eat at once. *Serves 4*

Last spring photographer Joyce Oudkerk Pool and I found a piadina truck at the side of the road outside of Bologna. The piadina is made fresh every morning for lunch and again in the afternoon for evening customers. Sandwiches are then assembled to order throughout the day.

prosciutto and mozzarella on a poppy seed roll

While mozzarella made with buffalo milk is rich and wonderful, it is also a bit watery for a sandwich. Use fior di latte, mozzarella made with cow's milk, for better results here.

4 poppy seed rolls

Mayonnaise for spreading

4 thin slices prosciutto di Parma

*3 ounces fresh cow's milk mozzarella cheese,
sliced ¼ inch thick*

Split the rolls and spread them with mayonnaise. Assemble each sandwich with a layer of prosciutto and a layer of mozzarella. Cut in half and serve.
Serves 4

primi

fresh fava bean, pancetta, and yellow pepper soup

In Tuscany, spring is the time for eating raw fresh fava beans with pecorino cheese. By early summer, the beans have toughened up a bit and are delicious in this soup.

1 pound fava beans, shelled

¼ cup extra-virgin olive oil

2 ounces pancetta, finely diced

1 onion, finely diced

1 carrot, peeled and chopped

1 celery stalk, finely diced

4 cups chicken stock (page 106)

4 large yellow bell peppers, halved, seeded, and deribbed

Salt and freshly ground black pepper to taste

In a medium saucepan of salted boiling water, blanch the beans for 1 minute. Drain and immerse immediately in ice water. Remove the skin from the beans by pinching off the end and squeezing the brightly colored beans out.

In a large stockpot, heat the olive oil over medium-high heat. Add the pancetta, onion, carrot, and celery and sauté, stirring constantly, for 4 to 5 minutes, or until golden brown. Remove a few pieces of the pancetta for garnish; transfer to paper towels to drain. Add the stock to the pot and bring to a boil. Add the peppers and decrease the heat to low. Cover and simmer for 30 to 35 minutes, or until the peppers are very tender. Purée the pepper mixture with an immersion blender or transfer in batches to a blender and process until smooth. Add the fava beans and simmer, uncovered, for 10 minutes. Season with salt and pepper.

Ladle the soup into warmed bowls, garnish with the reserved pancetta, and serve at once. *Serves 4*

warm farro salad with garden vegetables and salame

Farro is an ancient strain of wheat with a high protein content and a nutty flavor.

It can be found in health food and gourmet food stores in the whole grain, cracked, or as flour.

This dish can be served warm as a winter side dish or chilled for a summer salad.

2 cups whole farro

3 tablespoons plus ¼ cup extra-virgin olive oil

4 green onions (including 1 inch of the green parts), chopped

2 cloves garlic, minced

1 zucchini, diced

1 red bell pepper, seeded, deribbed, and diced

2 cups chicken stock (page 106)

1 cup canned chickpeas

4 ounces spicy salame, diced

Grated zest and juice of ½ lemon

Salt and freshly ground black pepper to taste

Romaine lettuce leaves for garnish

Soak the farro in water to cover for at least 1 hour, or up to overnight.

In a large, heavy saucepan, heat the 3 tablespoons olive oil over medium-high heat. Add the green onions, garlic, zucchini, and bell pepper and sauté until softened, about 2 minutes. Add the stock and bring to a boil. Drain the farro and add to the pan, cover, and decrease the heat to a simmer. Cook for 30 to 40 minutes, or until the farro is tender and stock has been absorbed. Stir in the chickpeas and salame. Cover and set aside to keep warm.

In a bowl, whisk the lemon zest, lemon juice, and the ¼ cup olive oil together. Season with salt and pepper.

Fluff the farro with a fork. Stir the dressing. Serve warm or chilled, garnished with a leaf of lettuce. *Serves 6*

pasta with chickpeas and pancetta

This is a classic winter dish, which is also often made with cannellini or borlotti beans. Chickpeas, also known as garbanzo beans, are called *ceci* in Italian. Canned chickpeas work well in the recipe and give a nutty flavor and good texture.

1 cup dried chickpeas

2 cloves garlic

7 sprigs rosemary

3 tablespoons extra-virgin olive oil

3 ounces pancetta, diced

1 onion, finely chopped

1 carrot, peeled and finely chopped

1 celery stalk, finely chopped

8 cups chicken stock (page 106)

1 tablespoon minced fresh flat-leaf (Italian) parsley

6 ounces short tube pasta of your choice

Salt and freshly ground black pepper to taste

Pick over and rinse the chickpeas. In a medium bowl, combine the chickpeas, garlic, and 1 of the rosemary sprigs. Add water to cover and soak overnight. Drain the chickpeas, reserving the garlic and rosemary.

In a large, heavy saucepan, heat the oil over medium heat. Add the pancetta, onion, carrot, and celery and sauté until golden brown, 6 to 8 minutes.

Add the stock, drained chickpeas, and reserved garlic and rosemary. Bring to a boil, then decrease the heat to a simmer. Add the parsley and cook, uncovered, for 1½ to 2 hours, or until the chickpeas are tender. Add the pasta and cook for 8 to 10 minutes, or until the pasta is al dente.

Discard the rosemary and season with salt and pepper. Ladle the soup into warmed bowls and garnish with the remaining sprigs of rosemary. *Serves 6*

pancetta-laced cannelloni with pesto balsamella

This cannelloni can be assembled a day ahead.

Make a double batch and freeze half of it for a quick dinner in the future.

Filling

12 ounces boneless veal

2 tablespoons extra-virgin olive oil

3 ounces pancetta, finely chopped

1 carrot, peeled and finely chopped

1 celery stalk, finely chopped

1 onion, finely diced

Pesto

2 cloves garlic

1 cup loosely packed fresh basil leaves

¼ cup pine nuts, toasted (see page 107)

¼ cup extra-virgin olive oil

¼ cup grated Parmigiano-Reggiano cheese

Balsamella Sauce

2 tablespoons extra-virgin olive oil

¼ cup finely chopped onion

3 tablespoons all-purpose flour

3 cups milk, warmed

Sea salt and freshly ground white pepper to taste

Fresh pasta dough (page 107)

¼ cup grated Parmigiano-Reggiano cheese

To make the filling, put the veal in a food processor and pulse until finely chopped. In a large sauté pan, heat the olive oil over medium heat. Add the pancetta, carrot, celery, and onion and cook until browned, 8 to 10 minutes. Add the veal and cook for 4 to 5 minutes, or until the meat is no longer pink. Set aside to cool.

To make the pesto, with the machine running, drop the garlic into the food processor. Add the basil and pine nuts and process to a grainy texture. With the machine running, gradually add the olive oil to form a smooth paste. Fold in the cheese by hand.

To make the balsamella, heat the olive oil in a sauté pan over medium-high heat. Add the onion and sauté for 3 to 4 minutes, or until softened but not browned. Decrease the heat to low and add the flour. Cook for 3 minutes, stirring constantly. Add the milk and simmer, stirring constantly, until thickened, for 3 to 4 minutes. Stir in the pesto and season with salt and pepper. Add 1 cup of the balsamella sauce to the meat mixture and set aside.

Using a pasta machine, roll the pasta dough to the second-thinnest setting. Cut the strips into twenty 3 by 4-inch rectangles. Set aside on a lightly floured work surface. In a large pot of salted boiling water, cook the pasta until barely tender. Do not overcook. Transfer to a large bowl of cold water to cool. Drain and place on a clean dish towel until ready to use.

Preheat the oven to 400°F. Lightly oil a 9 by 13-inch baking dish. Spoon a thin layer of the balsamella sauce in the bottom of the dish.

To assemble the cannelloni, place 2 or 3 heaping spoonfuls of the meat mixture on the long edge of one of the pasta rectangles. Roll the rectangle into a cylinder and place in the prepared baking dish, seam side down. Repeat with the remaining pasta and filling, packing the rolls snugly into the dish. Cover the rolls with the remaining balsamella sauce. Sprinkle with the Parmigiano-Reggiano and bake for 20 to 25 minutes, or until the cheese has lightly browned. Serve at once. *Serves 6*

penne, prosciutto, and artichokes

In Italy, the tiny violet artichokes called *carciofi violetti* are tender and can be eaten whole.

Baby artichokes are good substitutes; be sure to remove tough outer leaves.

12 baby artichokes, tough outer leaves removed

1 lemon

¼ cup extra-virgin olive oil

2 cloves garlic, sliced

Salt and freshly ground black pepper to taste

1 pound penne pasta

4 ounces thinly sliced prosciutto di Parma, cut into thin strips

Freshly grated Parmigiano-Reggiano cheese for serving

Cut off the tops and stems of the artichokes. Cut the artichokes in quarters lengthwise. Squeeze the lemon into a bowl of water, add the artichoke quarters, and let them stand in the lemon water until ready to use.

In a medium sauté pan, heat the oil over medium heat. Drain all but 8 of the artichoke quarters and thinly slice them crosswise (reserve the unsliced quarters in the lemon water). Add the garlic and sliced artichokes to the pan and sauté until golden, 4 to 6 minutes. Season with salt and pepper. Set aside and keep warm.

In a large pot of salted boiling water, cook the pasta and the remaining artichokes until the pasta is al dente, 8 to 10 minutes. Drain and toss with the sautéed artichoke mixture. Transfer to a warmed serving platter, garnish with the prosciutto, and serve the Parmigiano-Reggiano alongside. *Serves 4*

bucatini all'amatriciana

Amatriciana sauce comes from a town called Amatrice, in the province of Rieti in the region of Lazio (at one time, it was part of Abruzzo). This sauce uses a pancettalike product made from the pig's cheek and the jaw below the throat. In Amatrice, they would not use onion or garlic.

½ cup extra-virgin olive oil

8 ounces pancetta, diced

1 onion, diced (optional)

1 peperoncino (small dried red pepper),
or red pepper flakes to taste

½ cup dry white wine

4 ripe tomatoes (about 1 pound), peeled,
seeded, and chopped (see page 107)

Salt and freshly ground black pepper to taste

1 pound bucatini pasta

Grated Pecorino Romano cheese for serving

In a large skillet, heat the oil over medium-high heat. Add the pancetta, onion, and *peperoncino* and cook for 4 to 6 minutes, or until the onion is golden. Add the wine and stir to scrape up the cooked bits from the bottom of the pan. Cook the wine until evaporated, 6 to 8 minutes. Add the tomatoes and cook until slightly thickened, 10 to 12 minutes. Season with salt and pepper. Set aside and keep warm.

In a large pot of salted boiling water, cook the pasta until al dente, 8 to 10 minutes. Drain the pasta and add it to the skillet. Toss with the sauce over medium-high heat to heat through. Serve at once, with the cheese on the side. *Serves 6*

risotto with grilled sausages

This is an excellent way to use leftover grilled sausages.

Grilled vegetables also make a nice addition.

6 fresh pork sausages (about 1 pound)

Olive oil for brushing

7 to 8 cups chicken stock (page 106)

¼ cup extra-virgin olive oil

½ cup finely chopped onion

3 cups Arborio or Carnaroli rice

1 cup dry white wine at room temperature

2 tablespoons unsalted butter

½ teaspoon minced fresh rosemary

Salt and freshly ground black pepper to taste

Prepare a hot fire in a charcoal grill or preheat a gas grill to medium-high.

Lightly brush the sausages with oil and prick with a fork. Place on the grill rack and cook, turning once, for about 5 minutes on each side, or until nicely browned. Transfer to a plate and let cool. Cut into 2-inch diagonal pieces. Set aside.

In a large saucepan, bring the stock to a simmer over medium heat. Decrease the heat to low and maintain at a low simmer.

In a large, heavy saucepan, heat the ¼ cup oil over medium heat. Add the onion and sauté until softened, 4 to 5 minutes. Add the rice and stir for 3 to 4 minutes, or until the grains are well coated with oil and translucent. Add the wine and stir until completely absorbed.

Begin to add the simmering stock ½ cup at a time, stirring frequently to prevent sticking, until the stock is almost completely absorbed (but the rice is not dry on top) before adding the next ½ cup. Reserve ¼ cup stock to add at the end. Continue until the rice is tender but firm, 18 to 20 minutes.

Add the sausages and heat through. Turn off the heat and stir in the butter, rosemary, and reserved ¼ cup stock. Season with salt and pepper and serve at once. *Serves 6*

insalate e
contorni

bresaola, Parmigiano, and pear salad

If making this dressing one day ahead, taste and adjust the seasoning with vinegar before serving.

2 tablespoons balsamic vinegar

1 large clove garlic, minced

¼ cup extra-virgin olive oil

Salt and freshly ground black pepper to taste

½ cup sliced red onion

*4 ripe, firm pears, peeled, cored, and
cut into lengthwise slices*

4 cups mixed salad greens

2 ounces bresaola, cut into julienne

*2 ounces Parmigiano-Reggiano cheese,
shaved with a vegetable peeler*

In a bowl, whisk the vinegar and garlic together. Gradually whisk in the olive oil. Season with salt and pepper. Add the onion and let stand for at least 20 minutes or up to overnight in the refrigerator.

When ready to serve, add the pears and greens to the dressing and toss well. Serve garnished with the bresaola and cheese. *Serves 4*

fennel salame and fresh fennel salad

The fennel seed in finocchiona salame marries well with fresh fennel. Mince a little of the fresh fronds for garnish. If you can also find fennel pollen or fennel flowers, either makes a nice condiment for this salad; sprinkle on just before serving.

1 large fennel bulb, trimmed and finely sliced

4 ounces finocchiona salame, diced (or your favorite salame)

2 tablespoons red wine vinegar

¼ cup extra-virgin olive oil

Salt and freshly ground black pepper to taste

4 butter lettuce leaves

In a bowl, combine the fennel and salame. Pour the vinegar into a bowl. Gradually whisk in the olive oil, then the salt and pepper. Drizzle over the salame and fennel and toss well. Serve at once on top of each of the lettuce leaves. *Serves 4*

radicchio salad with spicy salame and sun-dried tomatoes

This winter salad will warm you up.

For a fresh variation, substitute diced pears for the sun-dried tomatoes.

3 cloves garlic, minced

2 tablespoons fresh lemon juice

½ cup extra-virgin olive oil

Salt and freshly ground black pepper to taste

2 ounces spicy salame, cubed

8 oil-packed sun-dried tomatoes, drained and cut into julienne

Leaves from 4 heads radicchio, torn into bite-sized pieces

3 ounces Parmigiano-Reggiano cheese, shaved with a vegetable peeler

In a salad bowl, whisk the garlic and lemon juice together. Gradually whisk in the olive oil. Season with salt and pepper. Add the salame and tomatoes and stir well. Add the radicchio and toss until well coated. Sprinkle the Parmigiano-Reggiano over the salad and serve at once. *Serves 4*

peas with prosciutto

This spring side dish is refreshing with grilled or roasted meats.

4 tablespoons unsalted butter

1 small spring or green onion, sliced
(including 1 inch of the green)

2 cups fresh or thawed frozen green peas

14 ounces thinly sliced prosciutto di Parma,
cut into thin strips

Salt and freshly ground black pepper to taste

In a medium sauté pan, melt the butter over medium heat. Add the onion and sauté for 3 to 4 minutes, or until softened but not browned. Decrease the heat to low and stir in the peas. Cook for 3 to 5 minutes, or until the peas are tender. Stir in the prosciutto and season with salt and pepper. Serve warm. *Serves 4*

green beans and pancetta

This is wonderful tossed with pasta. Chilled, it makes a fresh and delicious luncheon salad.

1 pound green beans, trimmed

3 tablespoons extra-virgin olive oil

3 ounces pancetta, thinly sliced

4 spring or green onions
(including 1 inch of the green part),
thinly sliced

Salt and freshly ground black pepper to taste

In a large pot of salted boiling water, blanch the beans for 1 minute, or until bright green. Drain and immerse immediately in ice water to stop the cooking. Drain and set aside.

In a large, heavy sauté pan, heat the olive oil over medium-high heat. Add the pancetta and cook for 6 to 8 minutes, or until lightly browned. Add the onions and cook for 3 to 4 minutes, or until the onions are softened and the pancetta is crisp. Add the beans and toss to coat well and warm through. Season with salt and pepper. Serve at once. *Serves 4*

sautéed broccoli rabe with pancetta, garlic, and mushrooms

If you are lucky, you might find fresh porcini mushrooms in your market in the fall.

If not, substitute your favorite seasonal mushroom.

1 pound broccoli rabe

3 tablespoons extra-virgin olive oil

½ cup chopped onion

2 ounces smoked pancetta, diced

3 cloves garlic, sliced

Pinch of peperoncino (red pepper flakes)

6 ounces shiitake mushrooms, sliced

½ cup dry white wine

Salt and freshly ground black pepper to taste

In a large saucepan of salted boiling water, blanch the broccoli rabe for 1 minute. Drain and immerse immediately in ice water. Drain and set aside.

In a sauté pan, heat the olive oil over medium-high heat. Add the onion, pancetta, garlic, and *peperoncino* and sauté until the onion is softened but not browned, 3 to 4 minutes. Add the mushrooms and sauté for 3 to 4 minutes, or until softened. Add the wine and broccoli rabe and continue to cook, stirring frequently, until the wine has reduced and the rabe is tender, 4 to 5 minutes. Season with salt and pepper. Serve at once. *Serves 4*

sformato di Parmigiano and prosciutto

Here is an elegant but simple side dish that can accompany roasted or grilled meats.

A *sformato* is a dish that is cooked in a mold, then unmolded to serve.

8 slices prosciutto di Parma

3 tablespoons extra-virgin olive oil

½ cup diced onion

¾ cup milk

4 eggs

1 cup (4 ounces) grated Parmigiano-Reggiano cheese, plus ¼ cup shredded cheese for serving

⅛ teaspoon freshly grated nutmeg

Preheat the oven to 375°F. Lightly oil four ½-cup ramekins. Line each with prosciutto, leaving an end to extend 1 inch above the top of the ramekin.

In a medium sauté pan, heat the olive oil over medium heat. Add the onion and sauté for 3 minutes, or until softened but not browned. Add the milk and heat until small bubbles form around the edges of the pan. Remove from the heat and let cool.

In a bowl, beat the eggs. Stir in the 1 cup grated cheese, the milk mixture, and nutmeg. Pour into the prepared ramekins. Fold the extra prosciutto over the top. Cover the ramekins with aluminum foil and place in a baking dish. Place the dish in the oven and pour in hot water to come halfway up the sides of the ramekins.

Bake for 35 to 40 minutes, or until a knife inserted in the center of each custard comes out clean. Invert onto individual serving plates, sprinkle with the ¼ cup shredded cheese, and serve at once. *Serves 4*

secondi

Most butcher shops sell pig casings. If the casings are fresh, rinse them in water with a little salt and vinegar. If you buy them already dried and salted, soak them in water to cover for at least 20 minutes. Many stand mixers have a sausage attachment for filling the casings with the ground meat mixture. Otherwise, a sausage funnel is indispensable. You can also use a pastry bag with a wide tip to fill the casings. See the Resources on page 108 for sources to buy casings.

homemade sausage

Fresh sausage is easy to make at home. Once stuffed, the sausages will keep in the refrigerator for up to three days or for up to one month if frozen. The ultimate cooking method for the sausages is grilling, but the ground mixture is also delicious used as a stuffing.

1 pound pork butt or shoulder, coarsely ground

2 tablespoons fine sea salt

2 tablespoons fennel seeds, crushed

1 tablespoon coarsely ground black pepper

30-inches of natural pig casing, soaked and drained

In a large bowl, combine the pork, salt, fennel seeds, and pepper and mix well.

Slide the casing onto the stuffing tube. Tie with kitchen twine at the end to close securely. Gently but firmly, push the pork mixture into the casing so that there are no air pockets. Do not overstuff; the sausage should be soft to the touch. Tie at the end to close securely. Place the sausage on a work surface. Twist the casing and tie it with string about every 4 inches, twisting in the opposite direction each time. Pierce the sausages with a needle to release any air bubbles. *Makes 6 sausages*

winter stew of salumi and cannellini beans

This winter warmer freezes well, to be reheated when the chill is deep in your bones.

1 cup dried cannellini beans

6 tablespoons extra-virgin olive oil

2 ounces pancetta, diced

1 onion, chopped

1 carrot, peeled and chopped

1 celery stalk, chopped

4 cups veal or beef stock (page 106)

3 fresh sausages, cut into 1-inch chunks

1 red onion, cut into 1-inch chunks

1 pound potatoes, cut into 1-inch chunks

8 ounces portobello mushrooms, stemmed and quartered

10 cloves garlic

1 tablespoon coarse sea salt

1 cup dry white wine

4 ounces salame, diced

½ cup oil-packed sun-dried tomatoes

1 teaspoon minced fresh thyme

Salt and freshly ground black pepper to taste

Rinse and pick over the beans. Soak the beans in water to cover overnight.

In a stockpot, heat 3 tablespoons of the olive oil over medium-high heat. Add the pancetta, onion, carrot, and celery and sauté for 6 to 8 minutes, or until lightly browned. Add the stock and bring to a boil. Drain the beans and add them to the pot. Decrease the heat to low and simmer, covered, for 1½ hours.

Preheat the oven to 400°F. In a Dutch oven or large flameproof casserole, combine the sausages, red onion, potatoes, mushrooms, garlic, and the remaining 3 tablespoons olive oil. Toss to coat well and sprinkle with the sea salt. Place in the oven and roast for 45 minutes, or until the sausages and vegetables are browned.

Remove the pan from the oven and place on the stove top over high heat. Add the white wine and stir to scrape up the browned bits from the bottom of the pan. Cook for 6 to 8 minutes, or until the wine is almost evaporated. Decrease the heat to low. Add the cooked beans and their liquid, salame, sun-dried tomatoes, and thyme. Continue to simmer for 25 to 30 minutes, or until the beans are tender. Season with salt and pepper. Ladle into warmed bowls and serve at once. *Serves 6*

onion, sausage, and apple tart

This savory tart can be served in small slices as an appetizer or in larger portions as a main course.

Pastry

1¼ cups all-purpose flour

½ teaspoon salt

½ cup (1 stick) cold unsalted butter, cut into teaspoon-sized pieces

4 to 5 tablespoons ice water

Onion and Apple Filling

⅓ cup extra-virgin olive oil

2 large red onions, thinly sliced

8 ounces fresh sausage (page 91), casings removed

½ cup apple juice

1 Rome apple, peeled, cored, and sliced

1 cup milk

2 eggs

1 teaspoon ground coriander

⅓ cup grated Parmigiano-Reggiano cheese

To make the pastry, in a food processor, combine the flour and salt. With the machine running, drop in 1 piece of butter at a time, processing until evenly distributed. Pulse, adding the water, just until the dough comes together. Do not overprocess, or the dough will be tough. Place in plastic wrap and flatten into a disk. Refrigerate for at least 1 hour. To make the pastry by hand, see method on page 107.

Preheat the oven to 350°F.

On a lightly floured work surface, roll the dough out to a thickness of ¼ inch. Press the dough into an 8-inch springform pan with a removable bottom. Line with parchment paper and fill with pastry weights or dried beans. Bake for 35 minutes, or until firm. Remove the weights and parchment and place the pan on a wire rack to let the pastry cool slightly.

To make the filling, in a heavy, medium sauté pan, heat the olive oil over medium-high heat. Add the onion and sausage and sauté until lightly browned, 8 to 10 minutes. Add the apple juice and stir to scrape up the browned bits from the bottom of the pan. Bring to a boil and cook until the liquid is reduced slightly, 10 to 15 minutes. Add the apple to the pan, decrease the heat to low, and simmer until the apple is just softened, about 6 to 8 minutes. Remove from the heat and let cool.

In a small bowl, beat the milk, eggs, and coriander together. Stir into the apple mixture and pour into the pastry shell. Top the tart with the Parmigiano-Reggiano.

Bake for 40 to 45 minutes, or until the cheese is golden brown and a knife inserted in the center comes out clean. Transfer to a wire rack and let cool slightly before cutting. *Serves 8*

pancetta and grilled-vegetable frittata

A good addition to this frittata is diced salame. Mix it into the potato mixture just before cooking. This frittata can be made ahead and served at room temperature.

1 Japanese eggplant, quartered lengthwise

1 red bell pepper, seeded, deribbed, and cut into eighths

1 zucchini, quartered lengthwise

Extra-virgin olive oil for coating

Salt and freshly ground black pepper to taste

2 ounces pancetta, thinly sliced

6 eggs, lightly beaten

1 tablespoon minced fresh flat-leaf (Italian) parsley

¼ cup grated Parmigiano-Reggiano cheese

3 tablespoons extra-virgin olive oil

Prepare a hot fire in a charcoal grill or preheat a gas grill to medium-high.

Coat the eggplant, pepper, and zucchini with olive oil. Season with salt and pepper. Place on the grill rack and cook, turning once, for 3 to 4 minutes on each side, or until lightly browned. Transfer to a plate and let cool.

Preheat the oven to 425°F. Heat a medium non-stick sauté pan over medium heat. Add the pancetta and sauté for 5 to 7 minutes, or until crisp. Using tongs, transfer to paper towels to drain.

Chop the grilled vegetables into bite-sized pieces. In a medium bowl, combine the vegetables, eggs, parsley, and cheese and mix well.

Add the 3 tablespoons olive oil to the same sauté pan and heat over medium heat. Pour the egg mixture into the pan and cook for 3 to 4 minutes, pulling up the edges and tilting the pan to allow the uncooked eggs to run underneath, until the eggs just begin to set. Decrease the heat to low, cover, and cook until a knife inserted in the center comes out clean, about 6 to 8 minutes. Invert the frittata onto a serving platter and cut into quarters. Serve at once, topped with the crisp pancetta. *Serves 4*

polenta with vegetables and salame

Create your own combinations of seasonings for the polenta; leftover grilled vegetables and sausages are also delicious. The polenta can be served hot or chilled. Once it has chilled, it can be cut into squares and grilled or reheated in the oven.

2 tablespoons extra-virgin olive oil

4 cloves garlic, minced

8 ounces button mushrooms, sliced

1 eggplant, peeled and cut into ¼-inch chunks

2 tablespoons minced fresh flat-leaf (Italian) parsley

Salt and freshly ground black pepper to taste

4 ounces salame, diced

4½ cups chicken stock (page 106)

1½ cups polenta

Preheat the oven to 375°F. Lightly oil a baking sheet.

In a heavy, medium sauté pan, heat the oil over medium-high heat. Add the garlic and sauté for 2 to 3 minutes, or until softened but not browned. Add the mushrooms and eggplant and cook for 6 to 8 minutes, stirring occasionally, until the liquid has evaporated. Add the parsley and season with salt and pepper. Stir in the salame and remove from the heat.

In a large, heavy saucepan, bring the stock to a boil over medium-high heat. Gradually add the polenta in a fine stream while whisking constantly. Decrease the heat to medium and continue to cook, stirring constantly, for about 20 minutes, or until the polenta easily comes away from the side of the pot. Stir in the salame mixture.

Transfer the polenta to the prepared pan, spreading it evenly and smoothing the top. Bake for 15 minutes, or until heated through. Remove from the oven and cut in squares to serve. *Serves 4*

prosciutto, fig, and garlic pizza

There couldn't be a more heavenly combination than figs, roasted garlic, and prosciutto.

Pizza Dough

1 envelope active dry yeast

2 tablespoons sugar

1½ cups warm water (105° to 115°F)

3½ cups unbleached all-purpose flour

½ cup semolina flour

1 tablespoon salt

3 tablespoons extra-virgin olive oil

2 heads garlic

4 tablespoons extra-virgin olive oil

Salt and freshly ground black pepper to taste

1 cup (4 ounces) shredded mozzarella cheese

6 ripe, firm figs, quartered lengthwise

12 slices prosciutto, cut into ½-inch-wide ribbons

To make the pizza dough, in a medium bowl, dissolve the yeast and sugar in ½ cup of the warm water. Let stand until foamy, about 10 minutes. In the bowl of a heavy-duty mixer fitted with a dough hook, combine the all-purpose flour, semolina flour, and salt. With the machine running, add the yeast mixture and oil, then gradually add the remaining 1 cup water. Knead for 10 minutes, or until the dough is smooth and elastic. Transfer the dough to a lightly floured work surface. Knead the dough into a ball, then transfer to a lightly oiled bowl. Turn to coat the dough, cover, and let rise in a warm, draft-free place for 1 hour, or until doubled in volume.

Punch down the dough and divide into 6 pieces. Form the pieces into balls. Cover with a damp towel and let them rise for 45 minutes, until doubled in volume.

Preheat the oven to 500°F with a pizza stone inside.

Oil a small roasting pan. With the tip of a small knife, score around the center of each head of garlic; do not cut into the cloves. Remove the top half of the papery skin, exposing the cloves. Place the heads in the prepared pan and pour 2 tablespoons of the olive oil over each. Season with salt and pepper, cover, and bake for 20 minutes, or until the cloves are soft. Remove from the oven, leaving the heads covered, and let cool to room temperature. Squeeze the garlic pulp out of the cloves into the olive oil remaining in the pan.

To assemble the pizzas, stretch each ball of dough to a round about ¼ inch thick and 8 inches in diameter. Place each round on a flour-dusted pizza paddle to assemble. Rub the dough lightly with some olive oil from the roasted garlic. Sprinkle with the mozzarella, figs, and roasted garlic, spreading to cover the surface but leaving a ½-inch border.

Slide the pizzas onto the pizza stone and bake for 4 to 5 minutes, or until golden brown. Remove from the oven, add the prosciutto, and serve at once.

Makes six 8-inch pizzas

pork loin wrapped in pancetta

In addition to adding flavor, the technique of wrapping with pancetta helps

to tenderize and moisten lean cuts of meat.

*1 boneless pork loin, trimmed
(about 2 pounds)*

Salt and freshly ground black pepper to taste

3 ounces thinly sliced pancetta

*2 Granny Smith or pippin apples, peeled, cored,
and shredded*

1 clove garlic, thinly sliced

1 teaspoon minced fresh sage

6 tablespoons extra-virgin olive oil

1 cup dry white wine

2 pounds potatoes, quartered

Preheat the oven to 400°F. Lightly oil a roasting pan.

Split the pork loin lengthwise without cutting completely through so that it can be opened like a book. Pound lightly with a wooden mallet to an even thickness of about 1 inch. Season with salt and pepper.

Place half of the pancetta on the pork loin in a thin layer. Top with a layer of apple and sprinkle with the garlic and sage. Fold the meat over the stuffing; cover the loin, especially at the seam, with the remaining pancetta; and tie with kitchen twine at 2-inch intervals.

In a large roasting pan, heat 4 tablespoons of the olive oil over medium heat. Add the pork loin and cook for 4 to 6 minutes, turning, until browned on all sides. Add the wine and stir to scrape up the browned bits from the bottom of the pan. Cook for 6 to 8 minutes, or until the liquid has evaporated.

Add the potatoes to the roasting pan. Drizzle the remaining 2 tablespoons of the olive oil over the loin and potatoes. Place in the oven, pancetta side down, and roast for 35 to 45 minutes, or until an instant-read thermometer inserted in the center of the loin registers 160°F. Transfer the meat to a cutting board and let rest for 5 minutes. Slice crosswise and arrange the slices on a warmed serving platter along with the potatoes. Serve at once. *Serves 6*

saltimbocca

This is a quick dish to prepare after a long day at work. A classic in Rome, *saltimbocca* literally means "hop in the mouth," referring to the lively flavors of this dish.

4 veal cutlets (about 1¼ pounds total)

8 thin slices prosciutto

8 fresh sage leaves

3 tablespoons extra-virgin olive oil

1 clove garlic, minced

1 pound spinach, stemmed, washed, and chopped

Salt and freshly ground black pepper to taste

3 tablespoons unsalted butter

Juice of 1 lemon

Roll the veal between 2 pieces of parchment paper with a rolling pin until flattened to an even thickness, about ⅛ inch. Cut each piece in half.

Place a piece of prosciutto on top of each piece of veal. Top each with a sage leaf and fasten the layers together with a toothpick.

In a large, heavy sauté pan, heat the olive oil over medium-high heat. Add the garlic and sauté for about 2 minutes, or until softened but not browned. Add the spinach and sauté until all of its liquid has evaporated, about 5 to 7 minutes. Season with salt and pepper. Transfer to a warmed serving platter and keep warm.

In another large, heavy sauté pan, melt the butter over medium heat until it foams. Add the veal and cook, turning carefully once, until lightly browned, about 1 minute per side. Add the lemon juice to the pan and stir to scrape up the browned bits from the bottom of the pan. Season with salt and pepper to taste, place on top of the spinach, drizzle with the pan drippings, and serve at once. *Serves 4*

chicken stuffed with sausage and spinach

This filling is also delicious stuffed into a whole chicken and roasted.

4 whole boneless, skinless chicken breasts

4 ounces fresh spinach, stemmed, steamed, and squeezed dry

1 pound homemade sausage (page 91), casings removed

½ cup whole milk ricotta cheese

1 clove garlic, minced

Salt and freshly ground black pepper to taste

3 tablespoons extra-virgin olive oil

1 cup dry white wine

2 cups chicken stock (page 106)

Place the chicken breasts between 2 sheets of plastic wrap. With a wooden mallet, pound to flatten the chicken breasts to an even ½-inch thickness.

Chop the spinach finely. In a medium bowl, combine the spinach, sausage, ricotta, and garlic and mix well. Spread evenly onto the chicken breasts, leaving a ¼-inch margin. Season with salt and pepper. Roll the chicken lengthwise and tie securely with kitchen twine.

In a roasting pan, heat the oil over medium-high heat. Add the chicken rolls and cook, turning, for 6 to 8 minutes, or until browned on all sides. Add the wine and stir to scrape up the browned bits from the bottom of the pan. Cook for 4 to 5 minutes, or until the liquid has evaporated. Add the stock. Decrease the heat to low, cover, and simmer for 30 minutes, or until chicken is opaque throughout and the liquid has thickened. Transfer to a cutting board and let cool slightly. Using a sharp knife, cut the chicken crosswise into ½-inch-thick medallions. Transfer to a serving platter and spoon some of the cooking juices over the chicken to serve. *Serves 8*

peppers stuffed with rice and salame

This traditional recipe is usually made with green bell peppers, but the plate really comes alive visually when you use red and yellow peppers.

2 large red bell peppers, halved crosswise, seeded, and deribbed

2 large yellow bell peppers, halved crosswise, seeded, and deribbed

3 tablespoons extra-virgin olive oil

1 onion, coarsely chopped

1 carrot, peeled and coarsely chopped

1 celery stalk, coarsely chopped

½ cup tomato sauce

2 cups cooked rice

1 tablespoon minced fresh flat-leaf (Italian) parsley

1 tablespoon minced fresh basil

½ teaspoon minced fresh oregano

½ teaspoon minced fresh thyme

Salt and freshly ground black pepper to taste

3 ounces spicy salame, diced

¼ cup grated Parmigiano-Reggiano cheese

In a covered steamer over boiling water, steam the pepper halves until softened but still firm, 4 to 5 minutes. Set aside to cool.

Preheat the oven to 400°F.

In a medium, heavy sauté pan, heat the olive oil over medium-high heat. Add the onion, carrot, and celery and sauté for 4 to 6 minutes, or until golden brown. Add the tomato sauce, rice, parsley, basil, oregano, and thyme. Decrease the heat to low and simmer, stirring occasionally, for 15 to 20 minutes, or until thickened. Season with salt and pepper. Stir in the salame, reserving a few pieces for the top.

Lightly oil a 9 by 13-inch baking dish. Place the peppers in the dish, cut side up. Spoon the rice mixture into the peppers. Sprinkle with the Parmigiano-Reggiano cheese and the reserved salame. Bake for 15 to 20 minutes, or until the cheese is golden brown. Serve at once. *Serves 4*

basics

chicken stock

One 3-pound chicken, cut up

1 carrot, peeled and cut into ½-inch pieces

1 stalk celery, cut into ½-inch pieces

1 onion, cut into ½-inch pieces

Bouquet garni: 1 sprig fresh parsley, 1 sprig fresh thyme, 1 bay leaf, and 4 or 5 peppercorns

1 gallon water

In a nonaluminum stock pot, combine all the ingredients and bring to a boil. Decrease the heat to a simmer and skim the foam from the top. Simmer for 2 hours, skimming occasionally. Let cool. Strain and refrigerate the stock overnight. Remove and discard the fat. Store in the refrigerator for up to 3 days, or freeze for up to 3 months. *Makes 5 quarts*

Note: Stock freezes very well. Try freezing it in 2- or 4-cup portions, to be used later in soups or sauces.

veal or beef stock

6 pounds beef or veal shank bones, cut into 3-inch lengths

2 onions, cut into 1-inch pieces

Olive oil for coating

2 carrots, peeled and cut into 1-inch pieces

1 celery stalk, cut into 1-inch pieces

Bouquet garni: 1 sprig fresh parsley, 1 sprig fresh thyme, 1 bay leaf, and 4 or 5 peppercorns

10 quarts water

Preheat the oven to 425°F. Put the bones and onions in a lightly oiled roasting pan and roast, turning occasionally, until very brown, 35 to 40 minutes.

In a large nonaluminum stockpot, combine the bones, onions, and all the remaining ingredients and bring to a boil. Decrease the heat to medium and simmer, uncovered, for 3 hours, skimming occasionally.

Strain the stock into another container and discard the solids. Let cool, cover, and refrigerate overnight. Remove the congealed fat. Store in the refrigerator for up to 3 days or freeze for up to 3 months. *Makes 5 quarts*

Note: Stock freezes very well. Try freezing it in 2- or 4-cup portions, to be used later in soups or sauces.

basics

pasta dough

3 cups unbleached all-purpose flour

4 eggs

1 tablespoon extra-virgin olive oil

Put the flour in a food processor. In a small container with a pour spout, whisk the eggs with the oil.

With the processor running, slowly add the egg to the flour until the dough starts to come away from the sides of the workbowl. Process for 30 seconds and check the consistency. The dough should be moist enough to pinch together, but not sticky. Continue to add egg until desired consistency. On a lightly floured surface, knead the dough to form a ball. Place in a self-sealing plastic bag to rest for at least 15 minutes.

Roll out one-fourth of the dough at a time, keeping the remaining dough in the plastic bag to avoid drying it out. Using a hand-cranked pasta machine, start on the widest setting. Put the pasta through 8 to 10 times, folding it in half each time until the dough is smooth. Continue putting the dough through the rollers, without folding it, using a narrower setting each time until the dough is semitransparent and very thin. Cut the strips of dough into the desired pasta shape. *Makes 1 pound*

Note: To make the dough by hand, mound the flour on a work surface. Make a well in the center and add the eggs and oil. With a fork, gradually blend the egg mixture into the flour. Knead for 10 to 15 minutes, or until smooth and elastic.

preparation tips

Toasting Pine Nuts: Spread the nuts on a dry baking sheet and toast in a preheated 350°F oven for 5 to 7 minutes, or until golden brown and fragrant.

Peeling and Seeding Tomatoes: Cut out the core of each tomato. Drop the tomatoes in a pot of boiling water and blanch for 30 seconds; transfer immediately to ice water to stop the cooking and release the peels, which will slip off in your hands. To seed, cut the tomatoes in half and squeeze out the seeds.

Roasting and Peeling Peppers: Place whole peppers directly over a high gas flame. If you do not have a gas stove top, use a grill or put the peppers on a baking sheet directly under your broiler. Turn the peppers frequently until blackened all over. Place them in a brown paper bag to steam and cool for about 5 minutes. Peel the peppers by scraping the blackened skin off with a sharp knife. Remove the stem and seeds before cutting as directed in the recipe.

Making Pastry by Hand: Combine the flour and salt in a large bowl. Cut the butter pieces in with a pastry cutter until the mixture resembles coarse meal. Add the water and mix to just bring the dough together. Knead on a lightly floured surface just until smooth. Wrap in plastic wrap and flatten into a disk. Refrigerate for at least 1 hour.

resources

domestic producers

It could be my California roots, or it could be the similarity in climate, but I think the best domestic cured meats in the United States come from the San Francisco area. In 1970, a group of San Francisco Italian-American producers of cured meats won the right from the USDA to cure meats in the traditional Italian way, complete with their inherent molds, and the right to call them "Italian salami" (the American spelling). Salame from Italy is not usually called "Italian salame," but will be marked "Made in Italy."

Armandino Batali, Salumi
Seattle, WA
www.salumiartisancuredmeats.com
Tel./fax (206) 223-0817
Handmade culatello, lamb prosciutto, lardo, hot soppressata, guanciale, pancetta, and several salamis.

Paul Bertolli, Oliveto
Berkeley, CA
www.oliveto.com
At the time of this writing, Bertolli is a few months away from offering his high-quality artisanal cured meats for sale. Check the website for updates.

Taylor Boetticher, Fatted Calf Charcuterie
Berkeley, CA
www.fattedcalf.com
Tel. (510) 301-9279; fax (510) 653-4327
At the Berkeley farmers' market. Local delivery in San Francisco Bay area for orders greater than $75. Traditional products using organic and all natural meats: fresh Italian-style pork-fennel sausage, guanciale, pancetta, finocchiona, bresaola, mortadella, and lardo.

Molinari's
San Francisco, CA
www.molinarideli.com
Tel. (415) 421-2337
San Francisco's first Italian-style salami company, since 1896, with a wide variety of Italian-style salumi.

François Vecchio
Columbus Salame Company
San Francisco, CA
www.columbussalame.com
Tel. (510) 429-6860
Classic Italian-style salumi. Also available from www.zingermans.com.

Ingredients and Supplies

If you decide to start making your own *salumi*, use high-quality ingredients and supplies.

Farm to Table
www.farmtotable.org
A wonderful East Coast website promoting sustainable farming. They hold that food "produced sustainably and regionally provides great quality, boosts our economy, protects our farmland, enhances our local food systems, and keeps us—and our environment—healthy." If you are thinking of curing your own meats, start with the best.

Niman Ranch
www.nimanranch.com
Livestock raised on sustainable land with humane treatment, natural feed, no antibiotics or hormones. A good source for ingredients to make your own. Also guanciale, lardo, sheep and hog casings, pancetta, and smoked salame.

Butcher & Packer Supply
www.butcher-packer.com
From meat hooks and casings to smokers and sausage stuffers.

Dean & Deluca
www.deananddeluca.com
Tel. (877) 826-9246; fax (800) 781-4050
In addition to prosciutto di Parma, they have a culatello produced in New York State, air-cured with juniper and seasoned with cracked pepper.

Rogers International, LLC
Portland, ME
Tel. (207) 828-2000
www.rogersintl.com
Carries Pio Tosini prosciutto di Parma.

D'Artagnan
www.dartagnan.com
Wild boar prosciutto.

Gustiamo
www.gustiamo.com
Excellent Internet source for imported Italian products.

Italian resources and producers

Culinary Arts
27 West Anapamu Street, No. 427, Santa Barbara, CA 93101
A traveling resource: Quick Guide to Italian Salumi, a regional listing of salumi with complete descriptions. Mail order only; $4.50 includes shipping in continental United States. Mail a check payable to Culinary Arts.

bibliography

Agriturismo Poggio Etrusco in Tuscany
Montepulciano (Siena) Italy
www.FoodArtisans.com
Holiday rentals at the author's farm.

Antica Corte Pallavicina and Ristorante
al Cavallino Bianco
Via Sbrisi, 2
Polesine Parmense (Parma)
Tel. (011-39) 0524.96136;
fax (011-39) 0524.96416
www.acpallavicina.com
*Producer of culatello di Zibello,
and an excellent restaurant and
farm to visit.*

Italian Food Artisans
Tel. (805) 963-7289
www.FoodArtisans.com
*Weeklong culinary workshops in
several regions of Italy.*

Made in Italy
www.madeinitaly.com
*At this website you can check product
codes to see if they are authentic
Italian-made products or counterfeits.*

Prosciutto di Parma
www.parmaham.com
*The official English-language site
for the consortium of prosciutto di
Parma.*

Prosciutto di San Daniele
www.prosciuttosandaniele.it
*The official site for the consortium of
prosciutto di San Daniele.*

Barberis, Corrado; Alison Leitch; and Orazio Olivieri. *Il Lardo di Colonnata*. Milano: Federico Motta Editore, 2003.

Bertolli, Paul. *Cooking by Hand*. New York: Clarkson Potter, 2003.

Bordo, Valter; Giacomo Mojoli; and Angelo Surrusca. *Salumi d'Italia*. Bra, Italy: Slow Food Editore , 2001.

Di Carpegna, C., et al. *Atlante dei Prodotti Tipici: I Salumi*. Rome, Italy: Agra Editrice, 2002.

Jenkins, Nancy Harmon. *The Essential Mediterranean*. New York: HarperCollins, 2003.

McGee, Harold. *On Food and Cooking: The Science and Lore of the Kitchen*. New York: Fireside, 1997.

acknowledgments

First, thanks go to my family for their patience and support. Next, my gratitude goes to Jennifer Barry, who is more than a collaborator; she is a friend and a muse, who not only conceived of this book but also helped it to take form in many ways. I also extend my appreciation to editors Holly Taines-White and Annie Nelson for helping to shape the final product. Thanks to Kimberly Wicks for her steady encouragement, and to Dario Cecchini, for opening his library to me.

David Biltchik and Sebastiano Brancoli were substantial resources with regard to understanding the legalities of imported meats.

Much appreciated are the *salumi* producers who opened their laboratories and shared their art with me. They include Raffaele Barbato and Giuliana Nese, Armandino Batali, Luigi Biggù, Vincenzo and Cesare Chini, my dear friend Federica de Gori and her family, Nicola Ghersetich, Fausto Guadagni, and Renaissance man Massimo Spigaroli. Thank you to Nano Morandi and Laura Galli at Hosteria Giusti and Massimo Bottura at Osteria Francescana in Modena for inspiration in the kitchen and at the table. Appreciation to Antica Enoteca Becaria and Gastronomia Volpetti for letting us shoot some great photos.

Kudos to photographer Joyce Oudkerk Pool, food stylist Pouké Halpern, and copyeditor Carolyn Miller. It is a delight to work with such a professional team.

Jennifer Barry Design thanks the following individuals and companies for supplying us with excellent meats for our recipe photography: David Biltchik of Consultants International Group, Washington, D.C.; Ruth Lowenberg of Lewis and Neale Agency, New York; Cheese Works West, Berkeley; and Lou Mascola of Molinari's, San Francisco. Thanks also go to food and photo styling assistants Terri Dien, Shana Lopes, and Chris Hu for their help with the recipe photography.

index